HELP ME!

I'M FAT!

By Lauren Wood

ISBN 978-0692620311
Published by Paradisiac Publishing

www.paradisiacpublishing.com

This book is dedicated to anyone feeling bad about personal appearances, regardless of what you look like. When you feel good about yourself you will be beautiful to yourself and anyone that matters in your life, and hopefully that will be a ton of people

If you come across anyone that feels differently, make sure you make their life hell…

Also, try your best to be nice to people even if you become a narcissistic asshole

Also, bottom line, no matter what you do to improve yourself or change your physical appearance, you can have different motivations, but at the end of the day you will be successful when you are doing it for yourself

Thanks so much to The Foundation in Davenport, IA and Moline, IL for giving me the tools to really take control of my life. I will be forever indebted to your grace. I'm so glad my success story is something you can use…
#mooselife

This book is mainly for women because I'm not sure men understand…

THE OLD TESTAMENT

THIS IS AN INTERACTIVE BOOK

Check out **www.quadcitycrossfitter.tumblr.com**

It has all the funny memes anyway and Microsoft Word is a nightmare to try and paste shit into

THE NEW TESTAMENT

Cluelessius 56:67

How to lose weight and feel better about yourself. Also weight loss does not necessarily equate feeling better about yourself, however these three steps will help you accomplish one or both:

1. Don't eat fast food even though it's easier and cheaper, you will pay for it later, BELIEVE ME! I cannot think of something that will fuck up your body worse than American fast food. Probably hard drugs and alcohol, for sure, but fast food is a god damn close third, I am both being and not being dramatic. Also you can eat cheap and super fucking healthy on the cheap. If enough people see this and give a shit I'll release another book explaining that.

2. Move your ass. It doesn't really matter what you do, you can dance the fuck around in your basement listening to Vampire Weekend if you want, if you are having fun and will stick with it, do it! I like Crossfit because it is extremely funny to me in so many different ways, plus hello, hot guys! Running is also cool, because I can listen to music. Basically equate moving your ass with something you enjoy and you will continue to do it.

3. Eat healthy for your body type. It takes awhile to figure that out and you have to reach out to qualified people who know what the fuck they are talking about to help guide you.

The Rest Of This Is For You To Take Notes On Your Own Journey

Keep at it!

You're doing great!

Awesome!

Don't give up!

How's it going?

Keep it up!

You are a rockstar!

You are crushing it!

Dominate!

Rock faces!

You are amazing!

Don't stop!

Keep pursuing your goal!

Do it up so hard!

Definitely you're getting close now, right?!

Fuck, what are you even doing?!

No, I am sorry you are on the right track!

Good job!

www.ingramcontent.com/pod-product-compliance
Lightning Source LLC
Chambersburg PA
CBHW070210100426
42743CB00013B/3127